Love 'n
Blessings

Thank you 🌑
the Support

Where's the Balance
IN TODAYS RELATIONSHIPS?

ALONZO TAYLOR JR.

WHERE'S THE BALANCE
IN TODAYS RELATIONSHIPS?

© 2021, Alonzo Taylor Jr.

All rights reserved. This book or any portion thereof may not be reproduced or used in any manner whatsoever without the express written permission of the publisher except for the use of brief quotations in a book review.

Paperback ISBN: 978-1-09836-792-3

Contents

INTRODUCTION	1
THE GUIDE	3
CHAPTER 1 "ARE YOU THE TOXIC ONE?"	6
CHAPTER 2 "DON'T GET EVEN JUST MOVE ON"	9
CHAPTER 3 "DOES YOUR PARTNER OPINION MATTER"	12
CHAPTER 4 "WANTS" VS. "NEEDS"	15
CHAPTER 5 "MAYBE YOUR TYPE IS THE PROBLEM"	18
CHAPTER 6 "INDEPENDENT DOESN'T MEAN MASCULINE"	20

CHAPTER 7 22
"LET A MAN BE A MAN"

CHAPTER 8 25
"IS PERSONALITY ENOUGH"

CHAPTER 9 27
"WHY HE WON'T MARRY YOU"

CHAPTER 10 30
"DON'T START WHAT YOU CAN'T FINISH"

CHAPTER 11 32
"REASONS WE MAY CHEAT"

CHAPTER 12 35
"WHAT'S HUSBAND/WIFE MATERIAL"

BONUS THOUGHTS 38
"ORAL SEX (FELLATIO)"

CONCLUSION 40

INTRODUCTION

First and foremost I want to take time to thank the creator for blessing me with the knowledge, and the talent that it took for me to even write this book. I also want to thank my friends and family who had faith that I would accomplish the things I said I would.

Let me give you guys a quick run down on what inspired me to write this book. Basically it was just watching my close friends, coworkers, and family members going through a divorce. It was also watching single parents who had to, or have to raise their children alone. I felt like I needed to put my two cents in, and maybe just maybe, I could help break the cycle.

I was raised with both parents in the household and it had a tremendous impact on my life. Both parents meant having positive role models around me, that I didn't want to disappoint, which lead me down the right path. All of those factors combined are what help mold me into the man I am today.

Over time our society has been able to destroy everyone's idea (thoughts or opinion) of what family is, and what it's like to have both parents in the household. In this day and age the new norm is being single and independent, and I find so many things wrong with this setup. One day it hit me and I was inspired to write this book in hopes of helping restore the BALANCE.

THE GUIDE

Before we get into the book I have 6 major traits that everyone should implement in their relationships. Those 6 traits are Communication, Support, IntimacyLove, Trust, and Respect.

<u>Communication</u> - Some couples have a hard time communicating with each other. This is not a good thing; you have to be able to open up to your partner about any and everything. My pops once told me that you could be mad at someone and they don't even know it. Now if you communicate with your partner and let them know what you're mad about, that situation can be resolved in a matter of seconds, I'm just saying.

<u>Support</u> – You have to be supportive of your partner. We all have a mission in life, some of us have dreams we want to achieve. Having a supportive partner can definitely make these goals a lot easier to accomplish. You wouldn't want to live your life with regrets or hatred towards your partner because they didn't support you or your dreams. One thing I'm certain of, is living a "what if " life isn't the way I would want to go.

<u>Intimacy</u> – In this department you have to keep your partner satisfied physically, mentally and emotionally.

    Intimacy really refers to how close you and your partner can become. I truly believe that you and your partner having a friendship/ relationship will build an unbelievable bond that can't be broken.

<u>Love</u> – As far as love goes you have to ask yourself, do you really love you? How can you love anyone when you don't even know how to love yourself? Loving you in my book means you don't tolerate mental, physical or verbal abuse of any sort. Loving you basically consists of your own well being and happiness. Always make sure that's first, and don't ever compromise that for anyone.

<u>Trust</u> – Without trust there's no relationship. Who wants to always feel imprisoned in a partnership? Every move you make, every step you take they're always watching you, because they don't trust you. Once you've broken trust it's very hard to repair. Honestly I feel that no matter what you do there's probably no chance of you gaining 100% of their trust back. Once you get to that point, there isn't really much to do but move on, sorry to say, but that's reality. People unfortunately can forgive, but it's HARD for them to forget.

<u>Respect</u> – Respect is not just given, it's something you must earn. Actually it kind of ties in with trust, the more a person can trust you, the easier it is for them to respect you. But remember you must earn it. Don't expect for anyone to just give it to you. In my eyes the best way to earn someone's respect is to show them your value (worth), by proving to your partner you have the qualities and traits that deserve their RESPECT.

CHAPTER 1

"ARE YOU THE TOXIC ONE?"

First, let's define TOXIC. The definition in the Dictionary reads adjective; 1) poisonous, capable of causing serious injury. 2) very harmful or unpleasant in an insidious way. Pay attention, because a closer look at the word makes it perfectly clear that the second syllable is pronounced SICK!

Think about the definition and a few questions come to Mind:

a.) Do you uplift and encourage your partner?

b.) Do you constantly degrade and discourage anything your partner attempts or does?

In these instances, do you work on a solution to what went wrong in the situation, or do you think you're always right?

Have you ever asked yourself if you are totally healed from past relationships and, you're confident that you've taken time to insure, your recovery? Are you carrying baggage from previous relationships, which lingered into your next?

If you identified with any of these scenarios, then toxicity may dwell in you. If you think that you shouldn't tell anyone how much you appreciate him or her, because you think they owe you something; you're the toxic one.

Here's an example: A man thinks that just because he pays the bills, and his wife takes care of her responsibilities, he doesn't have to recognize her contribution. WRONG! This is a catalyst, which leads to toxicity. It doesn't matter if its physical or mental abuse being exhibited, it still creates a toxic environment. If you enjoy inciting arguments, creating unnecessary drama, or becoming physically abusive as a solution, YOU ARE TOXIC!

I would advise that anyone NOT continue in these situations. You are in a no-win relationship, and couples are supposed to work as a team, not battle like gladiators. When we lose the focus of what a relationship is, it has deteriorated the balance.

How can you aspire to succeed at anything in life, if every time you take a step forward your partner holds you back? It's a proven fact that when people leave a toxic relationship, like magic they start to manifest dreams they've always wanted to achieve, but continuously had some type of obstacle. Toxicity is a virus that you don't want to infect your program.

Toxic people create stress, and stress can create other health related issues. Decidedly we don't need any unpeaceful thoughts in our life. The goal is to create and maintain BALANCE.

CHAPTER 2

"DON'T GET EVEN JUST MOVE ON"

I frequently hear my ladies say if he cheats on me, I'm going to get even. Ladies the only problem is, most men can't handle their women cheating on them, so they're not going to stick around long enough for you to get EVEN.

The point I want to get across is no one wins when your motive is to get even and not to get ahead. I understand how a situation like this could make you want revenge, but just remember revenge sex is not the way. Either forgive him and move forward or move on and forget.

Revenge sex can result in pregnancy, STD, or you just not liking the total package either way you are not winning so might as well not give up the BOX until it's worth it. If you can't handle the fact that your partner stepped out then don't take them back. You actually degrade yourself ladies when you tolerate anything less than excellence. And for you men, who actually will stick around, it's the same message for you.

Staying with her just to sleep with her best friend to make her jealous you could end up getting your windows busted out, could become baby mama #2 and so on. Like I say, were all adults and we should act in that manor. Going tit for tat with your partner usually ends up in a catastrophe.

Even if you stay with your partner after the fact if there isn't any trust there isn't a relationship. Honesty and Trust are the two main factors that build the bond (connection) and if either of those is broken you can kiss the relationship goodbye. So once again don't get even just leave and please don't drag your baggage with you into your next relationship. The best thing to do is give yourself time to heal so you can start over fresh; everyone you meet deserves an equal chance at your heart.

A good friend of mine gave me some advice that stuck with me and I would like to share it with you right now. Now we all know that men well some more than others have ego issues. The point I'm making is this; let's look at your box aka "The Cookie Jar" as if it were a garage. Unless that man has two cars' he's only looking for a one-car garage. His advice was if you happen to pull into the garage, and it's more like a two car garage, you may not want to be parking in that garage and that stuck with me.

Therefore ladies the idea is for a one-car garage because when your husband pulls in, he's going to want just his car to fit perfectly, nice and snug. Like I said before no one really wins in that situation, so just leave don't stick around to get revenge, plus whatever energy you put out that's the same energy you're going to receive. If you're being spiteful there's nothing good that could come from that because the intent wasn't good.

CHAPTER 3

"DOES YOUR PARTNER OPINION MATTER"

Let's consider if you thought for one second what your partner had to say doesn't hold any value, where would that lead to? Hypothetically speaking you and your partner are getting ready to buy a home together but you want a ranch style home, and they want a town home, what do you do in this situation?

Let's say you both wanted the same style of house but you want a man cave, and she wants her dream closet, now who wins this battle? Long story short your partner's opinion definitely matters if you are having a conversation, and your partner asked your opinion on how you would handle a particular situation. So now you have this great solution but since your opinion doesn't matter your partner turns around and asked several other people for their advice just for them to tell her the same thing you said day one.

I don't think you would appreciate that. Quite frankly no male or female wants a momma's boy, nor do they want a daddy's girl. Your Partner/Significant other wants, and needs to fill wanted, and by all means please keep friends and family out of your relationship, that's a disaster waiting to happen.

Now you can always ask questions about certain topics but don't ever air out your dirty laundry to friends and family. You never really know who's jealous or envious so keep things on the hush. And if you live with your significant other, as long you guys can come up with a final decision there's no need for anyone else's opinion.

Another thing to consider when you start taking outside advice you have to be mindful of who you are asking. I tell my friends and kids that it's important to watch who you hang around. If you want to be a doctor then all of your friends should be doctors, or nurses anyone in that field you're looking to explore.

If you are married or you're just dating and you need some advice, I wouldn't go searching through my single friends.

Sometimes your role model can make all of the difference on you making good decisions verses terrible ones. A lot of men and women seek advice from the wrong people, and that's a separate issue, but it can contribute to how and why your partner's opinions matter. You wouldn't ask a chef for advice on how to tune up your car? You would call a mechanic but you get my drift.

CHAPTER 4

"WANTS" VS. "NEEDS"

Now ladies you may not agree with what I'm about to say but it's definitely the truth. Some of you ladies want the man you don't NEED, but in reality, you need the man you don't WANT, let me explain. Most men that instantly take care of your wants can usually take care of another woman's wants. If he buys you an expensive purse, or expensive shoes, because he knows that makes you happy, he's definitely doing the same for another, trust me.

Now let's say you meet a man and the first thing out of his mouth isn't what expensive purse, shoes, or restaurant can he buy or take you too. If he always starts the conversations off by asking how are you doing today, is everything ok with you, then he sincerely cares. This is the type of man who will stop what they are doing to come to your rescue if you are on a flat tire, because he wouldn't be able to live with himself knowing you were stranded, and he did nothing about it. Let's say your faucet was leaking. He is the type of man that would come and try his best to fix it even if doesn't know a thing about plumbing. You see ladies, men with money don't mind spending it because he knows that's how to get the ladies.

One reason for that is because when he didn't have money, he didn't have the ladies, and that's not good either, but that's another topic. Basically, if that man is going to make sure you don't need for anything, eventually he will get you everything you want but only in that order, any other way is questionable. My children's mother once told me that all I do is pay ALL the bills and the car note as if I wasn't doing anything special.

She didn't understand that there are two types of men, and apparently she was more interested in the guy with time because my money wasn't good enough. Even though she didn't want for anything she didn't realize at the time the importance of what I was doing. Usually when a man or woman works hard to make sure their partner doesn't want for anything they genuinely care.

These are the type of people who elevate you, they will help you reach your goals, and anyone else would be more like a leech and they will just suck the life out of you. The point I am trying to make is watch your setups people, because they could be stopping you from accomplishing your dreams or achieving your goals. If your partner is holding you back that definitely will affect the balance in your relationship.

CHAPTER 5

"MAYBE YOUR TYPE IS THE PROBLEM"

Ladies, ladies, ladies, Fellas, fellas, fellas please stop choosing the same type of partner, then you act surprised when you receive the same results! In order for you to get different results, you have to do something different, think outside of the box.

What I would like for you ladies to know is there are basically two types of men. You have men with money and you also have men with time. It's very rare that you find a man with both. So first lets analyze your situation. Do you A.) Either want the man with lots of time, but no money to support or provide for you or B.) Do you want the man that can afford to wine and dine you whenever, on top of providing a roof over your head?

Everything has its pros and cons, but only YOU can decide what's best for you either way. Both men and women need to be supportive of their partner, that's part of being in a balanced relationship. If you chose to be with someone, you shouldn't mentally or verbally abuse him or her. No one deserves that kind of treatment. If the pros don't outweigh the cons, and you're still with that person, you've made your choice, so stick with it.

Listen fellas, stop being with women solely because of looks, and ladies stop being with men solely because of their status, if they don't physically and mentally complete you, then you are wasting your time. Now I can't let you off the hook like that. A lot of time we don't take a step back and look in the mirror.

If we were to start there then maybe we could see the problem clearly. Eventually after you've dated person after person after person you have to say, "Self maybe it's me with the issues". Since I'm the one with the issues what do, I need to do to fix it? Only after you realize who's the common denominator in the equation, is when you'll be able to solve it.

CHAPTER 6

"INDEPENDENT DOESN'T MEAN MASCULINE"

Well, first let me commend all the single parents taking care of home. It takes a lot out of you to maintain a household on your own, and I'm speaking from experience being that I'm a single dad raising two children on my own, so I know. Anyhow ladies fellas love a strong independent woman, but what we dislike are women who act or think they can handle a confrontation with a man.

Being strong just simply means being able to handle situations without folding. Basically being able to hold down your household without a man, and I'm not saying you don't need one because men and women definitely need that significant other. It's called a POWER COUPLE for a reason. It's only when the yin meets the yang that you achieve balance, and once you achieve it you have to maintain it.

Ladies you normally have a natural calming voice when you talk to us, so when you're yelling we forget who we're talking too. Instead of us going into a yelling match we need to have a civilized conversation with one another. In all honesty ladies you really could control a man and get what you want when you talk to us in that sweet, loving, caring tone you all have.

Your feminine side is where your power lies; believe me. Try this one-day, lets say your partner comes home and they are upset with something you've done. Try talking in that sweet, "I'm sorry baby it won't happen again" tone and watch what happens. I guarantee you a totally different result compared to you playing the blame game, instantly pointing the finger because you could never be wrong. Plus playing the blame game only shows how immature you still are.

Any adult knows that the only way to resolve a situation is someone has to take the responsibility for his or her own actions. Then and only then is when the problem can be truly corrected. Passing the buck only creates more problems it doesn't fix anything. Actually it takes a very strong and mature person to take full responsibility for their actions. So let's vow to not play the blame game any more and let's act like adults.

CHAPTER 7

"LET A MAN BE A MAN"

Ok Ms. Independent, I know you can handle it, as a matter of fact, we all know that you can handle it and we're proud of you. On that note you have to learn when to hold, and when to fold.

Prime example: You need your new TV Stand put together, so you call your man to take care of it for you. He comes over to put it together, but later he runs into some complications. Now do you A.) Run over there and show him how it's done, or B.) You wait until he leaves, and you fix it yourself, but you tell him your brother or uncle did it? If you chose A, we have a long way to go.

There's nothing wrong with a woman being able to fix something her man couldn't figure out. The only problem is us men have what we call EGO/ PRIDE and it's very delicate, so ladies please try your BEST not to shatter his because if your man doesn't feel needed, well let's face it, if either partner male or female doesn't feel needed they probably won't stick around in the relationship.

You can't pick and chose when you want the chivalry, or when you want to be treated equally, let me explain. When it's time to go out to eat or to a movie and the man says lets go dutch, I often hear responses like "He's cheap, he's not a real man, that's not how you treat a lady". My suggestion is we go back to the norm that worked backed then, and it can work right now.

We need to know our roles and stick with them. There are things that women naturally do better than men and vice versa. That's solely because we were designed to handle different tasks not the same ones. Diversity is what creates this place we call the universe.

Now I hear women say all the time, there are no good men left, but in reality they either don't know what a good man is, or they are intimidated by them. The women that say there aren't any good men may not really be looking, or they're actually content with the man they already have.

Digging a little deeper, men that have their stuff together tend to challenge these women who say there are no good men around, and most of the time they don't like to be called out or challenged. To them they don't want to feel weak, so they pick the man who doesn't have anything going on. These ladies are comfortable with these men because they're in control and honestly that's all some women want.

Some women have to be the one in control and the only way for them to achieve that is when they date these boys, then they turn around and say there aren't any good men left. Well hate to give you this spoiler alert, but ladies you weren't dealing with a man in the first place. My advice is ladies stop running from the challenge, because you may actually be running from your husband. Nothing that's worth having in life comes easy, so if a man challenges you, take the challenge; you may be surprised where you end up.

CHAPTER 8

"IS PERSONALITY ENOUGH"

I'm just going to be honest. It's hard to get pass the physical part, especially if you don't have to see that person daily. Have you ever just looked at someone, and said to yourself, "oh wow they look like they have a lovely personality?" Probably never. In my opinion it's the physical connection first, then it's the mental connection.

Now I will say that the mental connection will spoil everything. No man wants a stuck up ass female, nor does any woman want an arrogant ass man. So technically, both are extremely important, I'm just saying initially the physical part is going to get the ball rolling. I also read somewhere that we pretty much judge everything with our eyes here's an example.

If I were to put a red soda next to a blue soda you would choose the beverage that has the most appealing color to you. If you favor red over blue you would more than likely choose the red soda. You wouldn't say to yourself I wonder which one has the best flavor, you would assume that after you picked the color you liked. The same goes for food dishes, the one that seems more satisfying to the eye, is the one you're probably going to choose, regardless of taste.

So to make a long story short, I would say there are rare occasions that the personality would prevail, but I wouldn't exactly say it's enough. I know that there will be a lot of ladies debating about this. Let's be honest ladies you know good and well that if you have pass by guys that don't have on fresh gym shoes, or their outfit is dingy and not to your liking, you are going to pass him up.

Now I'm not saying that women or men won't date someone solely because of their personality. There are women who like men because they are funny and sweet and all that good stuff. There are also men who have dated women because they're down to earth; they are more understanding than most, and they like sports. So yes, there are times when personality is enough. What I'm saying is it's usually not the first attraction.

CHAPTER 9

"WHY HE WON'T MARRY YOU"

Let's dive right in. The first mistake a lot of women make is thinking, " I'm not doing that, I'm not his wife", or "I only do those things for my husband, so unless you trying to marry me", well you know the rest. Another deal breaker would be Ultimatums; "it's been 2 years, marry me or I'm leaving because you're wasting my time".

Now this can be dangerous because if he does take the deal and you get married, it could be 6 months to 6 years but more than likely it's a disaster waiting to happen. No one should ever be rushed into marriage, let nature take its course with that.

Another reason he's hesitant could be you're just not wife material to him, and he's just sticking around until he comes across a wife. Most men just like women who already know how far we're willing to go with the relationship, and we'll go as far as you ladies let us.

Now I'm not saying it's good for you to give him a ultimatum, but what I am saying is that laying out your expectations early in the relationship would help lower the assumptions.

<u>THE BREAKDOWN</u>

- WE ARE NOT MARRIED YET
- ULTIMATUMS
- YOU ARE NOT HIS TYPE

The main thing I see wrong with the "we are not married yet" statement is that's exactly why you are not married. Consider this, any time you get ready to make a big purchase like buying a car, or getting a house you make sure that you thoroughly inspect everything. You wouldn't dare buy a car new or used without test-driving it to see all it has to offer. Well, I hate to break this to you ladies, but it's exactly the same thing when it comes to marriage.

Ask yourself this, why would this man want, keyword WANT to marry me? And if you don't instantly have the answer that's exactly why he hasn't married you. Now about those ultimatums, no one likes ultimatums. Imagine you're hungry, you go to your favorite spot and before you could order the usual, they say tonight there are only two options.

Those are not to your liking, so you're probably going to leave and go somewhere you can get what you want. If a person isn't ready for marriage, I wouldn't force it on them, just let it happen, and only you know how long your willing to wait.

Now for you not being his type (wife material) just look at the signs. When you first meet someone of course everything is great. The thing is men are very simple, we don't ask for much. If you meet his mother and you're not at least doing as good, or three fourths of what she's doing you have a long way to go. Think about it, his mom is the first lady that shows him what loves feels like. He grows up seeing this love that he gets from his mother, so now that's the standard you ladies have to reach.

It's the same for the ladies, if that man doesn't have any of the qualities your dad has, you wouldn't even be interested. Not to say that everyone had both parents in their life but maybe they had a role model, or are just misguided. We all have certain qualities we look for in a husband or a wife, and nine times out of ten these traits come from the person, or persons we looked up to.

CHAPTER 10

"DON'T START WHAT YOU CAN'T FINISH"

If people were just honest from the jump things would be so much easier. Too often couples engage in a relationship under false pretenses. And let's be honest everyone's on his or her best behavior the first few months of the relationship. You get the good morning text, random phone calls throughout the day, flowers at work, social outings every weekend you know the works.

I like to think that whoever your soul mate, significant other or partner, whatever title you're comfortable with, you'll meet them on your daily routine. If you work a lot, read a lot, run in the park, go clubbing, skating etc.… More than likely you are going to bump into your partner in one of these locations. The good thing about this is that you won't have to change your daily routine, which will keep you from starting something you're not ready to finish.

Also remember you can't or at least shouldn't try to change anyone, so make sure who you are with is who you want to be with, and not just the idea of who you would rather have. If you don't like dancing, I suggest you don't go looking for a date at the club, because chances are they won't want to change their lifestyle for you.

Now if you love to read and you're at the local bookstore looking for a new book and you notice someone there, then that's the one you shoot your shot at. Basically if you meet someone at one of the places you love more than likely they're going to have a lot in common with you. The goal is NOT to start something YOU CAN'T FINISH.

CHAPTER 11

"REASONS WE MAY CHEAT"

I am by far not saying that it's ok or it should be tolerated, this is just my opinion on why some people cheat. First, I want to say that men and women cheat for different reasons. Maybe having an understanding of why someone cheated, would give you an edge on how to prevent that.

Most men cheat solely to see if they still got it. If the man stepped out it doesn't mean that he loves this girl, or he's going to leave so he can be with her, it's just that he has something to prove to himself. Honestly in some shape, form or fashion the man is unhappy to some level. Maybe his girl nags too much, maybe she's not supportive, or she doesn't cook. It could be a number of things, but either male or female we both need to feel wanted and respected.

As far as the ladies go if they start to even consider cheating they're half way gone anyway. Once most women start feeling that I'm being neglected vibe, it's pretty much over, especially if they come across a man that fills that void. In the previous chapter "Don't start what you can't finish", you literally can't stop doing what you've done to get the women.

If you start off writing little thoughtful notes, sending flowers, you know the wine and dine act, it's imperative that you continue what you've started. Basically men cheat based on a physical reaction, and women usually cheat off of an emotional reaction (someone's paying her some attention).

So fellas you better cater to your women, they say you don't miss something until it's gone. I believe that to be very true. Ladies I can't let you off the hook if you want to be treated like queens you have to treat your man like a king. You have to give respect to get respect. Ladies please start letting us men be men and stop dealing with these little boys and calling them men. If their mother didn't teach them how a man treats a woman it's definitely not your job to teach him.

Just a side note: ladies please stop thinking women are smarter than men when it comes to cheating, we just don't look. As soon as a woman has intercourse with a man the investigation begins. So of course anyone who's looking for something shall eventually find what they're looking for.

See once men get the prize so to speak, we think we're king-ding-a ling, and that the girl isn't going anywhere so we don't even bother to look. Now ladies please understand that men are not as stupid as you may think. If we notice our girl staying out later than usual suddenly, and wearing makeup and perfume everywhere they go, were going to notice the signs. Like I said before we don't pay attention, so we don't see it right away.

CHAPTER 12

"WHAT'S HUSBAND/WIFE MATERIAL"

So this is a very sensitive topic. Everyone has their own opinion about this because everyone grew up in different households. Naturally you only know what you grew up seeing. If you were fortunate enough to have both parents present you observed what they did, then constructed an idea of what your ideal wife or husband is.

As far as husband material, I would say the main traits would be he's a provider. I was raised that a man provides for his family. He always makes sure there's food on the table and a roof over our heads. A husband should also be a protector. It's a natural instinct for a man to protect his family. No woman wants a man she doesn't feel safe around and I don't blame her, she should feel like that.

Finally, I feel a husband should treat his wife like the queen she is. Now I don't necessarily believe in that happy wife happy life phrase. There's no way I'm going to waste my time on this planet making anyone happy, and it's not reciprocated, that just doesn't make sense to me.

Ok so as far as wife material, I feel like she definitely has to be a nurturer and it's only natural for her to do that. See lady's men also know whom they would want to have a child with. We do pay close attention to your mothering instincts. We want someone who's going to be a good mother to our children.

Second, we want a woman who knows how to be submissive, and I'm not saying this is one sided, as men are already submissive. Think about when it's time to pick a restaurant, or even what movie to watch you ladies usually make the final decision. We just want you ladies to be happy so we give you what you want. Any real man is going to make sure he takes care of your needs so I think we have the catering part down.

Now some fellas do lack in the sensitivity area (Romance) but that's another conversation. So, to reiterate what I was saying, women need to work on being more SUBMISSIVE. Society has changed the roles of both parties;

male and female, neither of us have the good old home training. Back in the day families lasted a lifetime, but look at all the divorces going on in today's age group.

Being a strong family use to be the thing, now all you hear is it's OK to be SINGLE, which it is, as long as it's by choice. Being single because you don't know how to treat the opposite sex is definitely not a good reason to be single and alone.

Being submissive is a huge trait and a great wife would support her husband the same as he should support her, but these are just a few things that in my opinion are great traits for a husband/wife.

Earlier in this chapter I stated that everyone's idea of the perfect partner would differ, but I believe you'll have a great starting point if you look for some of the traits I suggested. At the end of the day you should be with someone who makes you happy, they make you feel whole and complete.

It's always nice to be able to be yourself around your friends and family, so be sure to find a partner where you can be free to be yourself. Having solid people in your life can help you stay positive, and also help you reach your full potential NOW THAT'S BALANCE.

BONUS THOUGHTS

"ORAL SEX (FELLATIO)"

Now you'll know I couldn't write this book without touching on this topic. Personally, I can't speak on how fantastic it feels for the ladies, but I definitely can vouch for the fellas on this one.

Ok ladies I'm going to give you'll some advice you can choose to utilize it if you want. Imagine you have a teenager with a license, and you're going out of town for a few days. The teenager is supposed to be on punishment and is not allowed to drive your car anywhere.

So you have to ask yourself, if you were the teenager and there was a car sitting there with a full tank of gas would you drive it despite what your parents said? If you leave the gas tank on empty that teenager can't go anywhere, problem solved.

Now if you look at your husband/partner as the teenager you have to make sure he doesn't have a full tank before he leaves. Long story short fellatio for breakfast, lunch and dinner, the poor man won't be able to do nothing but think about the fellatio he received before he left. Therefore, that mans main focus will be on his partners actions the whole day. All because you occupied his mind at the beginning of the day.

Now fellas you definitely cannot be slacking in this department either. No one cares that you think you're king-ding-a ling, always remember, what one man won't do another one will, or what's one man's trash is another man's treasure. Don't lose your girl because you're not performing fellatio, you better get that bib or something and handle your business REAL TALK.

CONCLUSION

To summarize everything, I want to start off by saying if you're toxic or involved with someone who's toxic, PLEASE remove yourself from that situation. Being or dealing with toxic people is bad for your health, and the stress is a silent killer. If you take one lesson away from this book let it be that.

Toxicity is one of the main reasons relationships don't work. In my opinion each chapter has a valid reason on why most relationships don't work. Sure people cheat but why get even, when you can do one better and just move on. Remember, you need to value your partners' opinion and thoughts, and you have to show these people that you appreciate them, and you value their worth.

Maybe if you tried dating someone who's not normally your type you would get different results. Sometimes the prize can be right in front of you but if you're not looking then you won't see it. If we are ever going to restore the BALANCE in our relationships we must start with the root of the problem.

I tried my best to cover the main topics, well at least in my opinion these subjects need to be addressed that exists in a lot of relationships. Granted, I don't claim to be a relationship counselor, nor do I claim to have all the right answers. I truly feel my thoughts and opinion will help restore some much-needed BALANCE in most relationships.